JL41 3K

S0-CTX-662

Let's Read About Food

Milk and Cheese

by Cynthia Klingel and Robert B. Noyed
photographs by Gregg Andersen

Reading consultant: Cecilia Minden-Cupp, Ph.D.,
Adjunct Professor, College of Continuing and Professional Studies, University of Virginia

WeeklyReader.
EARLY LEARNING LIBRARY

**For a free color catalog describing
Weekly Reader® Early Learning Library's
list of high-quality books, call 1-800-542-2595
or fax your request to (414) 332-3567.**

Library of Congress Cataloging-in-Publication Data available
upon request from publisher. Fax (414) 336-0157 for the
attention of the Publishing Records Department.

ISBN 0-8368-3059-8 (lib. bdg.)
ISBN 0-8368-3148-9 (softcover)

This edition first published in 2002 by
Weekly Reader® Early Learning Library
330 West Olive Street, Suite 100
Milwaukee, WI 53212 USA

An Editorial Directions book
Editors: E. Russell Primm and Emily Dolbear
Art direction, design, and page production: The Design Lab
Photographer: Gregg Andersen
Weekly Reader® Early Learning Library art direction: Tammy Gruenewald
Weekly Reader® Early Learning Library production: Susan Ashley

Printed in the United States of America

1 2 3 4 5 6 7 8 9 06 05 04 03 02

Note to Educators and Parents

As a Reading Specialist I know that books for young children should engage their interest, impart useful information, and motivate them to want to learn more.

Let's Read About Food is a new series of books designed to help children understand the value of good nutrition and eating to stay healthy.

A young child's active mind is engaged by the carefully chosen subjects. The imaginative text works to build young vocabularies. The short, repetitive sentences help children stay focused as they develop their own relationship with reading. The bright, colorful photographs of children enjoying good nutrition habits complement the text with their simplicity and both entertain and encourage young children to want to learn — and read — more.

These books are designed to be used by adults as "read-to" books to share with children to encourage early literacy in the home, school, and library. They are also suitable for more advanced young readers to enjoy on their own.

— Cecilia Minden-Cupp, Ph.D.,
Adjunct Professor, College of Continuing and
Professional Studies, University of Virginia

I like to drink milk and eat cheese. They are good for me.

We choose from six different kinds of food. We need to eat all six kinds every day to stay healthy.

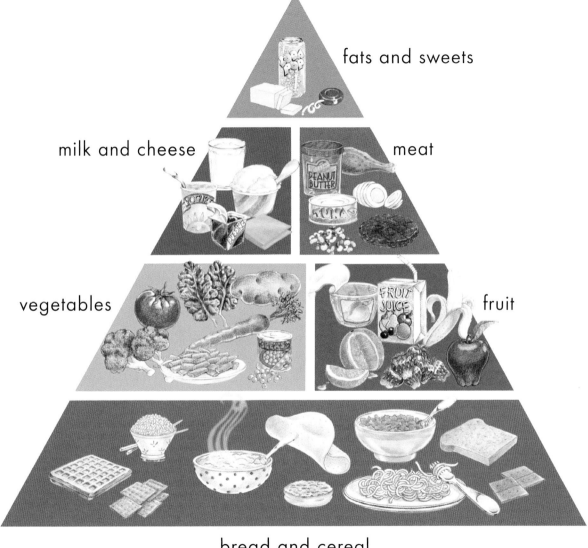

fats and sweets

milk and cheese

meat

vegetables

fruit

bread and cereal

My body gets vitamins and calcium from milk and cheese. Milk and cheese make me strong.

Most milk comes from cows. I love a cold glass of milk!

Yogurt is made from milk. Mmm, I like yogurt!

Cheese is made from milk. There are different kinds of cheese.

Some cheese is yellow. American cheese and cheddar cheese are yellow.

17

Some milk comes from goats. Goat cheese is white.

I am hungry for a cheese sandwich and a glass of milk!

Glossary

calcium—a soft, silvery-white element found in teeth and bones

vitamin—one of the substances in food that is needed for good health

yogurt—a thick, soft food made from milk

For More Information

Fiction Books

Babcock, Chris, and Mark Teague. *No Moon, No Milk*. New York: Random House, 1995.

Fleming, Candace, and S. D. Schindler. *Big Cheese for the White House: The True Tale of a Tremendous Cheddar*. New York: DK Publishing, 1997.

Hall, Donald, and Greg Shed. *The Milkman's Boy*. New York: Walker & Co., 1997.

Nonfiction Books

Llewellyn, Claire, and Helaine Cohen. *Milk*. Danbury, Conn.: Children's Press, 1998.

Pickering, Robin. *I Like Cheese*. Danbury, Conn.: Children's Press, 2000.

Web Sites

Got Milk?

www.got-milk.com/

For information about contests and games

Index

About the Authors

Cynthia Klingel has worked as a high school English teacher and an elementary school teacher. She is currently the curriculum director for a Minnesota school district. Cynthia Klingel lives with her family in Mankato, Minnesota.

Robert B. Noyed started his career as a newspaper reporter. Since then, he has worked in school communications and public relations at the state and national level. Robert B. Noyed lives with his family in Brooklyn Center, Minnesota.